BETTER SKIING

Bill Kent and Peter Roberts

BETTER SKIING

KAYE & WARD · LONDON
in association with Hicks, Smith & Sons
Australia and New Zealand

First published by
Kaye & Ward Ltd
21 New Street, London EC2M 4NT
1976

ISBN 0 7182 1448 X

Filmset in Monophoto Times by Computer Photoset Ltd
Printed in Great Britain by Whitstable Litho, Whitstable, Kent.

Contents

Foreword

Bill Kent, the co-author of this book, is a skier with over 30 years experience. He is a qualified instructor holding the ASSI Certificate of The National Ski Federation of Great Britain. He has done a lot of teaching on snow in Engleberg in Switzerland and on artificial ski slopes in England. His approach to skiing is to make it fun and interesting for the people he instructs, and he is always concerned that they are getting value for the money they spend. He has a sincere love of mountains and encourages his pupils to enjoy the mountains as well as their skiing. This book is written therefore from the practical point of view and I commend it to those concerned with school parties and introducing young people to this most exciting and exhilarating of sports.

Although Great Britain is a lowland country we have already produced ski racers who have achieved considerable distinction at International level, including The Olympics. They set the standard, but it is to the young people who are introduced to skiing by enthusiasts such as Bill Kent that we look to our International racers of the future.

Bill Kent is an Individual Life Member of The National Ski Federation of Great Britain, and I applaud his unselfish approach to skiing.

Ian Graeme.

Major General Ian Graeme, CB, OBE
Secretary, The NSFGB

Introduction — Skiing and Schools

Skiing is no longer a sport reserved exclusively for the wealthy 'international set' who spend their holidays in expensive resorts in the mountains amid snow and luxury. In the past few years organised package holidays have brought the snow slopes within the reach of millions from all walks of life, and today the skiing holiday has become an established family favourite with millions of Europeans.

Although skiing at any level of skill is tremendously enjoyable, and one of the most invigorating ways of exercising muscles that may not have had much opportunity for a work-out over the past months, most beginners who venture out on to the snow remain beginners. They never progress beyond the first few metres of the nursery slopes, never acquire more than the most rudimentary skills of skiing, never experience the real exhilaration of skiing, or discover the magic of the snow-clad mountains. It happens all too often to the people who 'go it alone' without previous experience, and who imagine that they can learn to ski without instruction. There is in fact no way of learning to ski without instruction. Attempting to do so merely invites accidents and disappointments.

School parties are a great opportunity for the young student to visit the snow regions. Backed by supervised pre-ski preparation, helped by reasonable costs, and with the vital advantage of being taught to ski by an expert instructor, the school party is one of the best ways to begin. A school trip to a ski resort introduces a youngster to a healthy and fascinating life and a thrilling sport — not perhaps as readily available as some others, but one that often captures the imagination of the schoolboy or girl so firmly that skiing becomes an important part of their leisure life in later years.

This small book is designed for the school library shelf. It is not intended to be a complete instruction course for the would-be skier, or comprehensive list of the many situations that present themselves to the skier with an L on his back, but more of an appetite-whetter for those who contemplate a school trip to the snow slopes and who wish to examine the project in more detail. A chapter for teachers will help in researching the organisational work, and the suggested further reading will prove more than useful when the teacher or party leader begins the actual count-down to the departure time.

The author and publishers would like to record here their thanks to Mr Alan Gibbon, MA, for his help, and his permission to publish extracts from his booklet *Going Skiing* which we consider essential reading for teachers intending to organise a school trip to a skiing resort. They also wish to thank E.R.O.S. (Educational & Recreational Overseas Service Travel [London] Limited) for permission to print part of their brochure; Mr Charles Christen of the Tourist Office at Engelberg in Central Switzerland, where most of the photographs were taken; Mr Teddy Amstutz, director of the Engelberg Ski School; Mrs Jacqueline Walter, instructor at the Engelberg Ski School and her son Christof, Miss Irene Muller also of the Engelberg Ski School, and the Alexandra Palace Ski Centre for their cooperation in allowing the use of their ski-slope.

The author would also like to thank the Swiss National Tourist Board for the use of the photographs on pages 11, 12, 16, 42, 74, 83, 84, 86 and 87; Thomson Holidays Ltd for use of the colour picture on the dust jacket; and Mr Doug Godlington for his kind permission to use his ski diagrams.

Bill Kent

1. Pre-ski Exercises

Expert skiers tell us that the sport is a leisurely exercise; that with training, the muscles of the leg and lower body accomplish automatically the balancing and direction-changing movements employed during skiing with little effort and no anguish.

However, to the beginner, skiing is an energetic and strenuous business with a lot of hard work to be done before enjoying the genuine thrill – and it is a great thrill – of skiing properly on the snow-covered slopes themselves.

Pre-ski exercises coupled with an artificial-slope course, will greatly speed up your progress on snow, and help to avoid those accidents which occur through trying to overload muscles unprepared for the new stresses of skiing. Regular exercise at home or at school for up to a couple of months before the holiday will pay enormous dividends.

Here are five suggested exercises. Increase the number of times each one is carried out as your fitness increases. The exercises should not exhaust you, though muscles that are not normally used in the way they demand will be a little stiff at first.

1. Stand with arms at sides, feet slightly apart. Swing arms back and drop to a crouching position, with heels still on the floor. Swing arms forward to an upright position; at the same time raise to full height. Repeat from six to twelve times, rhythmically.

2. Stand, hands on hips, with left foot three lengths in front of right. Bend

10

left knee, keeping the right leg straight with heel on the ground. Return to standing and repeat with right foot forward. Repeat six to twelve times.

3.   Crouch with heels off the floor and hands between knees touching floor, palms flat for support. Jump feet backward to full length, supporting weight on hands. Jump back to crouch position. Repeat six to twelve times.

4.   Stand, hands on hips. With weight on left leg, swing out right leg to right side as far as possible. Bring right leg down and swing it forward as far as possible. Repeat rythmically four times first with right leg then left leg. Repeat six to twelve times.

5.   Lie supine on floor, arms stretched beyond head. Sit up, bringing arms to grasp feet keeping knees straight. Heavier people may need to anchor feet. Lie down again with arms stretched. Repeat four to eight times.

6.   Run on the spot, not more than a hundred paces.

1. Skiing to school, old style. The original reason for skiing was simply to get from one snow-covered place to another.

2   3

2. A school ski party course on the slopes will not have this move in the syllabus! 'Hot-dogging' acrobatics are usually exclusive to those born in the snow-regions.

3. Typical lunch-break scene in the mountains above Engelberg in Switzerland.

4. Author and ski-instructor Bill Kent in a fast turn.

5. One down and four to go! A class practises kick-turns on an artificial slope in Britain.

4

5

2. Ski Clothing

Headgear

A woollen hat that can be pulled down over the ears is essential particularly when the pace of skiing gets faster. A cold wind knifing past exposed head and ears can be miserable and sometimes dangerous.

Anorak

Must be showerproof, comfortable, and a hood is more than merely useful if it snows or rains. Make sure that the shoulders are wide enough for the wearer to move arms about freely. An anorak should have snow or storm cuffs (tightly fitting inner cuffs) to keep wrists warm and to keep out snow. Heavy-weight garments are not necessary – quilted lightweight anoraks are sufficiently protective for the warm work the beginner will be doing on the slopes. Wind-proofing is more important than weight. Horizontal-topped pockets are best; forgetting to close an upright zip usually results in lost pocket contents.

Gloves or mittens

Nobody should ever ski without one or the other. Best is a combination of two types of covering, silk inner gloves with an outer warm mitten. Not many beginners manage this and most wear leather gloves, or mittens (which are warmer than fingered gloves). Avoid knitted gloves, which absorb wet snow. Use as long a glove/mitten as possible so that it overlaps the storm cuff at the wrist.

A good ski glove will have a strengthening piece between thumb and first finger fitted to combat wear caused by constant friction against the ski stick.

14

Ski pants

These are made of showerproof 'stretch' material (no true fabric is waterproof and this is not called for) and are as snowproof as possible. Today's ski pants are flared at the bottom (the change from the 'ballet' type pants to flared is not due to changing fashion but to the newer type of boots with higher sides). They have a stirrup on the foot on the inside of the lower part of the leg which fits snugly to the ankle and leg, and an outer slightly flared leg sewn on from just below the knee. The flared part goes over the boot, preventing snow from getting into the boot over its top. Pants are almost always hired by school parties and are usually 'unisex' style.

6. The well-dressed skier wears a simple ski anorak, flared ski-pants sun-glasses or goggles. This picture was taken in mid-April when the temperature was over 65 degrees Fahrenheit – but the young lady should have been wearing gloves.

Make sure that any pockets have working zips, or the novice will collect pocketsful of cold wet snow during falls on the slopes. Beginners should not attempt to wear jeans or other casual pants as they accumulate snow and water which can freeze into the material.

7. For the advanced skier (this is during a race) a hat and warm underclothing are a must – and goggles supplant sun-glasses.

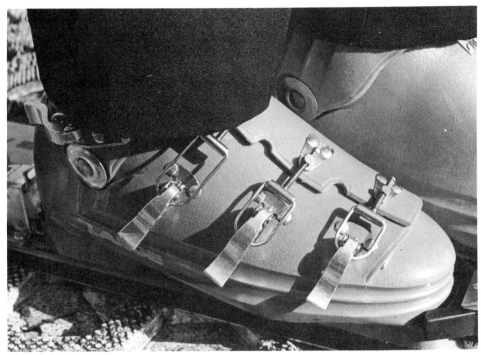

8. Flared ski-pants should protect the top of the boot, the inner lower-leg of the pants tucking inside the boot, with a stirrup around the instep of your foot.

Overtrousers and ski-suits

Lightweight proofed nylon or similar fabric trousers may be worn over jeans or long underwear, or over a pair of thickish pyjamas. Although they may be bought separately overtrousers are usually part of a complete ski-suit of similar material.

Underwear

'Long-Johns' are always useful in the snow, particularly for parties taking a ski-course during the Christmas holidays when the weather is usually colder. Silk is the best material, nylon the least suitable. A woollen vest is ideal, but it need not be a bulky garment. In the cold, two layers of thin clothes are always more effective than one thick layer. During the Spring months long underwear will not usually be necessary.

Socks

School parties tend to take any old socks. Football or hockey socks are *not* ideal as they have a raised knitted weave which eventually causes friction blisters. All ski shops stock special socks which have softly looped wool on the inner side for comfort.

Sweater

A light woollen high-necked sweater (not necessarily polo necked) may be worn over a shirt, or over a roll-necked ski shirt. Cotton T shirts are useful.

Goggles/sunglasses

Goggles are ideal but for beginners who spend just a single week on the snow, sunglasses will usually fit the bill. Plastic lenses of course. All-weather green-olive lenses serve a dual purpose combating the glare of the sun, and aiding vision in mist or fog.

Tour operators will usually suggest a local (UK) ski-shop from which the school party may hire ski-clothes. The most comprehensive 'ski-pack' supplied by a UK shop would comprise: anorak, ski-pants (hired and returnable) and goggles, mittens, socks, lunch-bag, woollen hat, rubber ski clips, lip-seal and sun-cream (purchased at a reduced price within the overall cost of the pack). The only items of equipment available for hire abroad are skis, boots and sticks.

3. Early Training

A party may arrive at the foot of the snow slope on the first day in one of two conditions. Completely ignorant of the principles and practice of skiing – or with many of the simple chores and techniques already learnt, and ready to launch into some of the basic movements on skis. School parties will be at a tremendous advantage if they have some knowledge of the fundamentals of dressing and equipping themselves and of the first principles of using skis on the snow, learnt on the artificial slopes at home. Time spent on one before going to the snow slopes is worth every hard grinding minute. It cuts down expensive and limited learning time at the ski resort – owing to the rise in all holiday costs schools now usually book just a one-week holiday, much too short a period to go through a full course of training leading to real enjoyment and proficiency on skis.

The sooner the party starts on the artificial slopes the better. September perhaps, when the places have been booked for a Christmas or even an Easter holiday, is the time to think of starting lessons. The normal school party course is usually five lessons (it may vary from region to region) and this should be preceded by pre-ski exercises at school. The boy or girl who wants to put more time in may take sessions of 'free' skiing on the artificial slope; i.e. without an instructor – or at least separately from the school group. At half-term many slopes charge reduced prices for children.

The school may wish to follow up the initial course with a second before getting to the snow (there is never any objection to this by pupils although parents may have a word to say about expense) and the benefits are significant.

When they get on snow, they will then find that they are promoted to the second or third class and begin immediately to be taught movements on skis. About a week of basic lessons on the snow can be saved this way – and if a school party has only a week at the resort that can mean a vast difference in the fun, to say nothing of accomplishment. And remember with just one week in the mountains, children do not normally get to the stage where they can ski reasonably well unless they have had prior training.

Artificial slope training

What do you learn on the artificial slope? Mainly the things that are a waste of time learning on the snow: how to carry skis; how to put on your boots (the resort school will not normally cover this, as when a party reaches the assembly point boots will have been put on). You'll learn how to put the boot into the ski binding (also a point not covered at the resort ski school), the length of stick to choose, how to hold a stick, how the boot should release from the binding in a fall, why the binding should be checked, and some of the basic skiing movements.

Here and in the next chapter are the main points of most artificial slope training.

9, 10. A four-clip boot, and (10) an economic three-clip boot of the type that will be seen more often on the snow in the future.

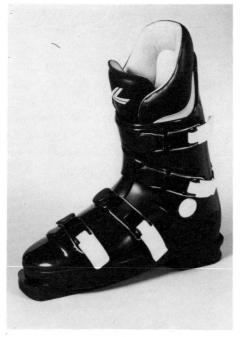

Boots: fitting and wearing

Modern ski boots are made of a fairly rigid plastic. Most are the four-clip type, a simplification of the more elaborate five-clip boot. And they need not be expensive – perhaps £25 will buy a pair that will last for half-a-dozen holidays. Correct size – only the wearer can decide that – is vitally important. It can be judged by the fact that when the boot is clipped up, the wearer's heel cannot move up and down more than $\frac{1}{2}$ an inch, (1·27 cm) but the toes can still be wriggled. And of course, that the boot is reasonably comfortable. Wear one pair of socks only when fitting (and when skiing) as two or three pairs set up a friction against each other and your feet. The modern ski sock is made of stitched looped wool and is available from most sports shops. They may also be worn for normal walking.

When trying on the boot make sure that the foot is well back and down into the heel of the boot. Then, clip up from the bottom, first on the loosest notch. If the boot is not tight (i.e. if your heel can move at all) clip into the next notches, again from the bottom. It is not necessary to have the top clip fastened too tightly on a dry slope although in snow it is important to fasten it more firmly. The most important buckle is the next one down, the one that pulls your heel down and backwards into the boot.

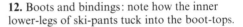

11. Checking that the heel does not move up and down inside the boot more than $\frac{1}{2}$ an inch.

12. Boots and bindings: note how the inner lower-legs of ski-pants tuck into the boot-tops.

The boot is the most important part of your equipment. Skis can be changed if they are too long or too short but you are stuck with your boots, once you are up on the mountain, particularly if you have brought them from home.

The beginner feels awkward in his boots at first and feels as though he is trying to walk on the moon. This, coupled with the fact that they are big, rigid and heavy, is because every boot is designed to keep the foot and ankle at a slightly forward angle, putting the weight on the ball of the foot, and to prevent any sideways movement of the ankle. Try walking like a big ape – it's much more comfortable!

Fitting the skis

Initially the boots will be fitted and tested on the ski at the hiring shop or depot. Modern skis are fitted with toe and heel bindings that release when put under strain from a fall. It is essential that novice skiers know how they work, and know that they *are* in working order. And it is most important that the teacher in charge of a school party is able to check that the release operates properly – and if only to avoid the situation where a member of the party tries to do it himself – wrongly. If the release mechanism is too loose the ski will snap off too readily. If it is too tight a fall will not release the ski and a leg injury is much more likely. It is not, however, the teacher's job to adjust bindings that may be incorrectly adjusted unless he has been fully instructed in the procedures. They should be taken back to the shop.

Before checking binding make very sure that the boot is fitting tightly on the foot, i.e. so that the heel cannot lift inside the boot. A heel that can move about inside a boot will more readily allow a strained tendon during a forward fall – or even during the forward movement when testing bindings. In effect the foot from the ankle down, the boot, the bindings, and the ski, should be one single unit.

The simplest 'forward' release check is to stand on level ground in boots and skis, making sure the boots are fitting well into the bindings. Put one ski forward a couple of feet, then jerk the rear foot and leg forwards, in a firm sharp movement, simulating a sudden fall. The rear ski should release the boot from the heel. There is also a sideways release for when a skier falls in such a way as to put lateral pressure on the boot. A check should be made by a second person by giving the boot a good thump with his fist on the side, or by the skier banging the heel of one boot against the side of the other. A strong bump should

22

knock the boot out of the binding. After satisfactorily checking the release, the number or colour of the setting should be noted and daily readings should be taken to make sure it has not been knocked off its correct tension.

13, 14. An instructor demonstrates the forward release check. The left foot-and-ski is placed ahead of the right . . . and the right foot jerked forward. The heel should release if the movement is sharp and firm.

Taking off skis

Skis are taken off in one of two ways, dependent on the type of binding. The most popular has a hole or depression on the back of the heel binding into which the point of the ski stick is inserted and pushed downward, opening the rear binding. The other type has the safety strap attached to the back of the heel binding which is pulled upward to open it.

A type of binding called the plate binding has been developed and may soon be seen on hired skis. The boot is permanently attached to a metal or plastic plate, which allows all the ski bindings at the hire point to be pre-set, and the adjustment made on the boot-to-plate fixture. The release mechanism operates between the ski and plate leaving the plate attached to the boot – a simpler and safer method.

A word about retainer straps which attach boot to ski. On the snow they are essential to prevent the situation in which a detached ski goes sailing off down the valley on its own after a fall. This, in some countries, is an offence against the law. On the artificial ski slopes straps are normally not fitted.

15. Taking off skis. This type of binding has a hole or depression at the heel to take the point of a ski stick. Push down firmly and the heel releases.

16, 17. Taking off skis. A strap attached to the back of the heel binding (it also doubles as the retainer strap) is pulled upwards to open the binding.

Ski sticks

At first beginners spend a fair part of their tuition time falling. The leather loop normally seen around stick handles can result in twisted fingers or thumbs so at the dry slope they are usually not provided. Learn to insert the entire hand through the loop when on snow, gripping the handle with the loop around the wrist, so that fingers don't get tangled up during a fall.

18, 19. The correct way to wear the loop at the top of a ski stick; i.e. keep your fingers out of the way.

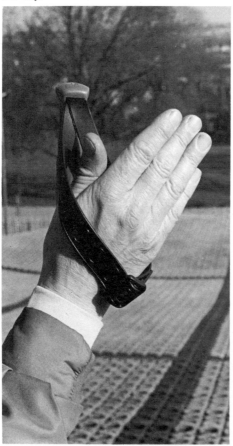 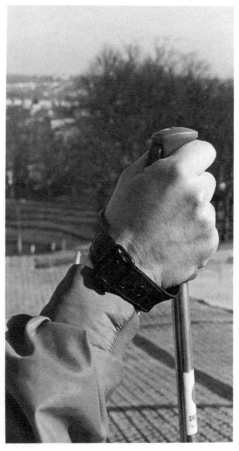

Carrying skis

Carrying skis can be dangerous – usually to other people. Don't carry them over the shoulder when inside a building or a cable car – hold them upright rather like the military shoulder-arms position. In the open carry skis over the shoulder at an angle of about 45 degrees (bound together with the rubber clips that should be provided) with the curved tips to the front. Many continental hire shops do not provide clips, and a school party organiser should check with the tour operator that they are supplied. Carrying skis without them can be awkward as they tend to 'scissor'.

20. Indoors or in a crowd (such as when queuing for a cable car, or packed into one) carry skis upright like this.

21. In the open skis are carried at about 45 degrees, tips down . . .

22. . . . *not* like this, which is one of the ways to break a window with them, or bang an unsuspecting neighbour's head.

Walking on snow (without skis)

On the hard-packed snow of the level approaches to the nursery slopes it is all too simple to fall flat on your face or back, planting your skis in someone else's way or digging them in his ribs. To walk safely – lean forward, spread your feet and walk leaning forward slightly. The forward-placing of your centre of gravity will keep you stable.

Putting on skis

At first a flat piece of ground will be chosen by the instructor for putting on skis. Later you will be shown how to put them on while standing on an incline, placing the skis horizontal to the fall of the slope. On the dry slope this is a simple exercise. On snow the ski will slide more easily and can upset balance – or vanish downhill if the strap has not been fastened. Standing below the parallel-placed skis, fasten the downhill ski first using it as a 'safety barrier' while putting on the upper ski.

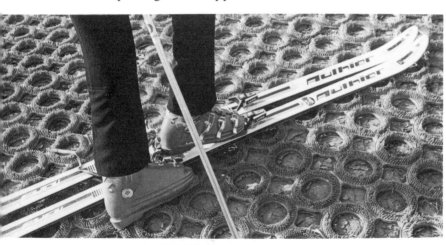

23, 24. Putting on skis. From a standpoint below the skis, put on the lower one first . . . then step into the higher one. The other way may allow the lower ski to go slithering down the slope. Whilst it may not be important on the artificial slope, it may disappear for ever in the snow.

Walking on skis

Firstly you will probably be given a few limbering-up exercises on the flat – lifting one knee up to balance on one ski for a few seconds, or flexing the knees to gain confidence. You will undoubtedly fall during these first few minutes on snow. Don't worry about it though – so will everyone else and your turn to laugh will come soon enough.

Skis must be kept parallel for stability when standing still and walking on the flat. Crossing the points or walking like a duck will quickly result in a fall.

Walking is simple. With parallel skis a wide handsbreadth apart, take long sliding steps, leaning into them slightly with bent ankles as you progress. Don't angle or lift the skis, just slide them forward over the snow (or plastic bristle of the artificial slope). Ski sticks are used as 'pushers' alternatively on .each step.

25. Walking on skis. Keep them parallel, take longish sliding steps. Lifting them only wastes energy.

Turning on the level

Facing the other way can be a problem at first. One of the simplest ways to turn around is the star turn. Keeping the back of the skis on the ground, move the front end of the right ski about a foot to the right (for a clockwise turn) closing up with the left. Continue these small radial moves and you'll turn in a circle. If you come across an immoveable object in the way, complete your turn by moving the rear end of the skis, leaving the fronts at rest. This turn may of course be done moving in the reverse sequence i.e. moving the heels round the clock first. It may also be used on an incline, to bring your skis facing the fall line to start a descent but must be 'braced' with the sticks as skis leave the horizontal.

30

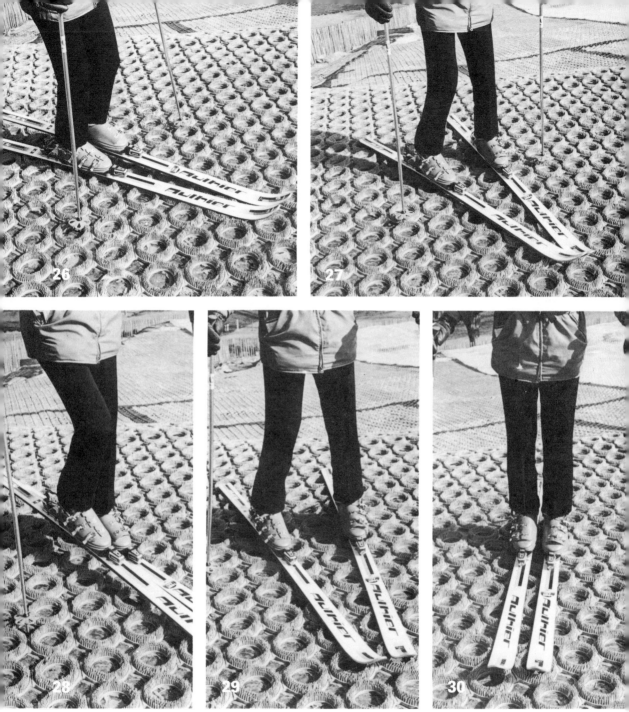

26—30. Star turning on the level, turning the heels and rear ends of the skis and keeping the fronts on the ground.

31—35. Star turn on a slope. Here a skier star turns into position to schuss down an artificial slope. From a horizontal ski position (31) she begins to star turn anti-clockwise, using the front ends of her skis and placing her sticks downhill. (32) When she takes up a more acute angle to the horizontal she begins to use the sticks as props to prevent a premature descent. When facing downhill (34) she brings the skis together taking up the position for a straight downhill run. (35).

34

35

4. On the Slope

This chapter deals with first movements in skiing. If the school party goes to an artificial slope for initial training these are the moves that will be taught in the short series of lessons. Here however, the movements are described as though they are carried out on snow, so that you will read 'place the stick in the snow' and so on. There is very little difference between the way they are described here and the method of performing them on the artificial slope, except that the plastic or bristle surface has very different characteristics to the snow surface at the resort. On the plastic-bristle slope for instance, edging the skis when using the braking effect of a snowplough would tend to force them to cross, whilst edging on snow would merely push the loose snow out of the way.

Walking up a slope

Method 1 – the side-step. With the skis horizontal i.e. at ninety degrees to the fall line, and the uphill ski half-a-boot-length in front of the lower, take small side-steps up the slope. As the slope gets steeper the knees should be angled into hill (i.e. 'edging' the skis) so that the skis do not slide sideways down-hill. At the same time the upper body should be held facing the valley (downhill) and leaning slightly out downhill – the forward position of the uphill leg will help in this. It is easier to side-step up a slope if you progress forward a little on each step, never trying to take too big a bite of the slope at a single step. It is vital to keep the skis horizontal (90 degrees to the fall line) to prevent them sliding forwards or backwards – the main error at this stage.

34

Method 2 is the herringbone, a faster way to climb, but more exhausting. Facing uphill, open the skis into a wide V and start walking uphill on the inner edges of the skis, taking care not to allow the rear ends to hit each other, or one to rest on the other. The ideal herringbone movement looks rather like a duck waddling uphill.

36. Walking uphill – the herringbone. Energetic but rapid, this is a method of walking up a short length of slope.

37. This rear view shows clearly that the skis are on their inner edges.

38. A young skier demonstrates the wrong way of herringboning. The back of the right ski rests on the other, 'nailing' the left ski to the ground.

After a fall

A fall is inevitable shortly after being introduced to an incline, and is no disgrace. Early falls are usually of the sit-down variety (use your bottom as the point of contact with the ground as much as possible in all falls). The easiest way to rise is to bring the skis into a horizontal (90° to fall line) position under the crouched body. Then put the one – or two – sticks into the snow on the uphill side, close to the side of the hip, and push yourself upright using them and your arms as levers. If the fall is untidy, rest on your side or back, swing the skis up into the air, bringing them down again on your downhill side and horizontally placed. Then get up. Never use your hands to break a fall on an artificial slope; fingers can catch in the cellular plastic surface and be injured.

39

40

41

42

43

44

45

39—45. Falls are inevitable, and the novice can find difficulty in getting back on his skis without instructions. If the fall is 'untidy', i.e. if the skis are uphill (39) or in a tangle, swing them up in the air, bringing them to rest parallel horizontal and on the downhill side (40). Bringing the body into a tight crouch over the boots, place the sticks in the snow near the uphill tip (41) and lever up (42 and 43) using one hand near the base and the other near the top of the sticks (there are times when only one stick need be used).

Schuss: straight downhill

This is the simplest ski movement. To turn into the fall line (see page 32) the star turn may be used, first placing the sticks in the snow on your downhill side and well away from the lower ski (which as yet is horizontal after side-stepping up to the point of descent). Star turn into your sticks using them and your fully extended arms as supports and brakes to prevent your running downhill until you are ready. The skis, now facing downhill are parallel and about eight inches apart. Your weight should be forward, pushing against the sticks, shins pushing against the top of your boots, bottom tucked in, and your slightly-bent legs flexible, ready to absorb the small undulations of the slope. Now let go . . . keeping that position, but with arms bent and sticks pointing backwards . . . and cruise gently downhill. Artificial slopes or nursery slopes should always have enough length to allow you to come to a natural stop on the flat, without plunging into the local stream. Don't at this stage bend down low as one sometimes sees skiers do to reduce wind resistance – you may feel you *need* all your wind resistance!

46, 47. Schuss: a straight downhill run. Here the skier uses and flexes the legs as she goes over the top of a small bump or mogul (46) . . . and straightens back into the schuss position to continue the run downhill (47).

Snowplough

Skiing instruction is ever-changing as new materials are developed allowing new techniques to be used, and ultra-short ski schools do not teach the snowplough. But it is a very necessary lesson for the beginner if conventional skis are to be used. The snowplough is primarily a method of braking for newcomers to skiing and is also used for teaching leading up to controlled turns, or is applied when skiing down narrow paths or gullies.

Facing downhill, using the sticks placed in the snow well in front of you as a 'parking' brake, spread the skis into a V with the points about six inches apart, knees slightly bent, hips and body weight forward. We've mentioned that skis are kept as flat as possible on the ground on a dry slope not 'edged' by angling the knees inwards, as the tips will cross. On snow they should be edged, pushing the snow away on your descent. This position will already slow your descent, and to brake further, push the heels out (i.e. push the back of the skis out and apart and out like a snow plough) keeping the front ends in approximately the same position. This way your descent can be slowed down to less than walking pace if you wish – for your entire downhill run – dependent on the

48. A slow, controlled descent in the snowplough position . . .

49. . . . and the snowplough stop, pushing the heels further out. The skis are edged in both snowplough pictures.

angle of the V formation of the skis. A very wide angle will result in a complete stop. The sticks should be held with hands about eight inches in front of hips and eight inches out from them, with the points well behind the body. If a fall becomes inevitable don't ever use the sticks to prevent it, and try not to fall forward using hands as an alternative brake – just roll sideways and fall naturally.

It should be remembered that the snowplough is a move learned by the beginner and used for controlled descent and turning in early lessons, but is used only rarely in normal advanced skiing. There are many other more efficient ways of doing both without employing the rather clumsy and exhausting stem, or snowplough.

50. Although snowploughing is a beginner's manoeuvre, it is useful as a control in certain circumstances for an advanced skier, such as on a narrow path where there is no lateral room to use other methods of braking or stopping.

51

52

51—56. The kick turn is another move that is useful to beginners and advanced skiers. It completely reverses the skier's direction and is done while there is no forward movement. It is used where there is no room to make a moving turn. With the skis parallel and horizontal, place the sticks into the snow on your uphill side and ski length apart. Lean back into the sticks keeping arms straight and in line with sticks (51). Lift the right ski up in front of you planting the rear end in the snow when it is vertical (52).

53

54

Let the upright ski pivot down on its end until it is parallel with the other ski, facing in the opposite direction (53). It sounds impossible but isn't. Pick up the left ski and swing it round until it is parallel with the other ski and facing the same way (54).

44

5

56

The ski sticks have been used for support and stability during these moves (55). Swing round to the new direction, bring the sticks back into normal use (56).

Snowplough turn

This beginner's manouevre looks inelegant, but later turns will be of a different type. Take up the snowplough position facing downhill, weight equally on both skis, and start the run. To turn left, increase the weight pressure on the right ski, by moving your body-weight over to the right advancing the right ski about half-a-boot length. The extra weight on the right foot will turn the right ski to the left and the left ski will run more freely, allowing you to turn left, still keeping in the knees-flexed snowplough position. Although it may seem against all your natural instincts during the left turn, the shoulders and body from the waist up must keep facing approximately downhill. If you allow your body to 'turn into the turn' you will find that the left turn continues until your skis are facing slightly uphill, and will start to run backwards. You must remember that, unlike taking a bend on a motor cycle, when you would lean *into* the turn, skiing demands an unnatural movement, that of leaning over to the *outside* of the turn, weighting the outside ski.

When learning on the artificial slope or on snow, familiarisation with turns is achieved by spending a complete lesson carrying out linked snowplough turns to the left, right, left, entering one turn directly from another, in a slow continuous sequence.

At the end of a turn you may want to move into a traversing position, in which the skis are parallel. The snowplough turn will have brought you naturally into a position except for the uphill ski which will still form the upper wing of the V. Since the downhill ski is bearing most of the weight, let the uphill one drift and close it up to the other.

58

57—59. Bill Kent leads a class down Alexandra Palace's ski slope in a series of snow-plough turns round poles, in a simple 'slalom' exercise.

59

60. Snowplough turn. From a snowplough position facing downhill the figure (2) bends his body to the left, putting weight on the left ski to turn to the left. Then a turn to the right (3, 4, 5) by weighting the right ski.

48

61. Snowplough turn principle: *(a)* Weight left ski turn right. *(b)* Weight right ski turn left.

62. On the snow slopes a class watches the instructor demonstrate the snowplough turn to the right.

63—65. These three photographs show the way the shoulders and hips are kept facing downhill. From a left traverse through a simple turn to an opposite traverse this skier demonstrates by the position of his sticks that his shoulders are facing downhill all the time. All the movement of the turning is done with the lower part of the body. It is not expected that a skier will be able to keep his shoulders facing *exactly* down the fall line – aim at keeping the upper body facing the valley as much as possible.

63

Traversing is moving across a slope at a sufficient downhill angle (from just a few degrees from the horizontal to almost directly downhill) to give you forward motion, with skis parallel. It is an alternative to a straight downhill run, where the slope may be too severe for the beginner, or the snow surface too difficult. In fact traversing back and forth across the wide nursery slope, linked by simple turns at each end is the way most beginners commence skiing, descending in a series of long zig-zags, and gaining confidence as they slowly traverse the piste executing perhaps half-a-dozen traverses and turns before reaching the bottom.

In the traverse position the upper ski is half-a-boot-length forward, with the body weight on the lower ski. Skis should be either together or only a

64

65

handswidth apart, though beginners will find the traverse more comfortable if they are spread a little further at first. Shoulders and hips will face naturally down the slope, approximately in line with the knees, which with the ankles are bent slightly and angled into the hill so that the skis are edged into the slope, preventing side-slipping. To counterbalance the thrust of the knees into the slope the top part of the body naturally leans the other way, downhill. The angle of traverse will dictate the speed, but a gentle traverse will allow the beginner to travel smoothly forward and gently downward at perhaps a brisk walking pace – which in any case will seem to be at a fast sprint to the novice! Braking can be done by using a small snowplough action, pushing out the heel of the lower ski, bringing the traverse nearer to the horizontal.

66, 67. Traversing; left and right. Note that the uphill shoulder is forward and the uphill ski leads. The sticks are kept to the rear out of the way.

68. The traverse position from the front (the hill runs down to the left) showing the skis edged into the hill, and the weight on the lower ski.

69. Bill Kent, on the Alexandra Palace ski slope in North London, demonstrates a traverse across a steep slope.

The side-slip enables the skier to slip his skis sideways down the fall-line of the slope, losing height whilst traversing. The ski may be slipped down the slope still keeping the line of the traverse, or they may be slipped to lessen the angle (or increase it), or to avoid an obstacle in the line of traverse. During traversing the skis are edged into the slope; to sideslip turn them so that the undersides are flat against the incline, keeping the skis closer together than during the traverse, and 80% of the weight on the lower ski. The skis will slip down until they are edged into the slope again.

Put weight on the heels when sideslipping if you wish to level out the descent of the traverse, on the front of the skis to increase the angle of descent. For the beginner the slide-slip is in some ways just an exercise in control, but is used to effect at a later stage in skiing.

70. Side-slipping. The skier has slipped her skis' edges by letting her knees roll out to the right (downhill) slightly flattening the bottoms of the skis allowing them to slip down the slope.

Swing turn

This is only slightly different from the snowplough turn, and is used at the end of a traverse to turn round into the next traverse. The swing turn is executed at a faster speed. Start a small stem with the upper ski (easy, as it is almost unweighted) and make a plough turn at the end of the traverse. Steer the skis round to the fall line by gradual weight on the upper (at the moment) ski, keeping it weighted and slightly behind the other ski as it becomes the lower ski, closing the unweighted (new) upper ski to the lower one, and giving a determined push of the heels of both skis to skid them round into the new traverse. As in all turns, your body above the hips should remain facing downhill as much as possible. The torso is in effect a balancing weight; the work of turning is done by the legs and hips.

71

72

73

71—75. Basic Swing Turn. From a left traverse (as the camera sees the skier) in the first picture, in which the weight is well forward and on the nearer (lower) ski, the right ski is pushed out in a small stem (72) and the left stick is being brought forward for the turn (73). The weight is now on the right ski and the swing to the left has started. In the next picture the stick has been planted and used to

74

75

slightly 'unweight' the skis as the skier turns (this use of the stick is optional in the stem turn) and all the weight is still on the right ski (74), with the left ski automatically closing to the right. Finally the skis are parallel again having completed the turn (75).

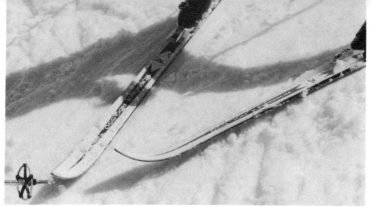

76. The outside ski (the instructor's stick points it out) should always lead slightly when making the stem turn.

77. The previous photo-sequence (71—76) has shown the movements of the skis during the swing or stem turn. Since they were photographed with the camera as the fulcrum they cannot show the changes of direction of the skier as she swings round. Here in diagram form is a swing turn sequence showing the turn from a traverse to the right through a right turn to an opposite traverse. In this turn the upper (left) ski is pushed out in a small stem and the body turned slightly down the slope, transferring weight to the left ski. The lower two drawings show the right ski – now the upper ski – being closed in to the left ski, coming into the traverse position.

78. The start of the swing turn to the right. Here the skier is pushing his left ski out into a small stem before starting to turn.

Uphill Christie

You have seen how to slow down or stop by snow-ploughing, but this is an inefficient method, particularly if you are moving quite quickly. The uphill Christie is a turn designed to bring you to a stop by parallel skiing. There are several variations of it but one of the simplest is this. From a traverse with, for example, your left side as the uphill side, you need to stop by turning your skis into the hill.

Immediately before the turn, straighten your legs and body, briefly unweighting the skis, then bend quickly down with knees angled into the slope, pushing the rear ends of the skis downwards by heels pressure, most weight still on the downhill ski. As the tips of the skis turn into the slope you ride to a halt on the uphill edge of the lower right ski. Keep your shoulders facing downhill as much as possible right to the end of the turn.

Parallel turns

A development of swing turning, this is another method of controlled descent, by a constant sequence of small turns, with skis parallel throughout.

Running in a fairly steep traverse position, start the turn by placing the lower stick in the snow slightly in front of the lower ski, and using it as a pivot to take the weight of the backs of the skis. Push the ankles out, skidding the skis into the opposite traverse using the same weight distribution as other types of turn but keeping the skis parallel. Immediately the shallow turn is made begin an opposite turn, using the other stick as a fulcrum. This requires some practice, particularly in timing, and is like constantly hopping round alternate sticks. In time the turns can be made more quickly so that each takes just a second and the skier is running downhill in a series of small flowing swings, completely in control.

5. Exercises on the Snow

Most exercises carried out in the snow will at first be under the supervision of the class instructor. They are done for several reasons; as limbering-up movements to tone up and flex muscles that may not yet have got out of bed; as exercises to familiarise the beginner with the feel of the skis and the snow; as ways of giving the novice confidence in his equipment and his balance. They should not be abandoned when you are not in a class. If you are on the slopes unsupervised, it's wise to start with some form of exercise – and to continue them whenever there is time to spare.

(a) One of the basic exercises is a sort of marching on the spot on skis. With the skis parallel bring one leg up at a time in a slow high marking-time action, keeping the raised ski parallel to its partner and the ground.
(b) Bring both skis up at the same time – a series of knees-raised jumps on the spot, still keeping skis parallel to the ground and each other.
(c) Sit down on the back of the heels – and get up again, without using hands or sticks.
(d) Jump both skis as in *(b)* but grounding them alternately on your left and right sides.
(e) From the skis-together stance, jump into the snowplough position, and back.

79, 80. Marching on the spot. Skis are raised alternatively in marching rhythm. Tips may be left on the snow or the skis kept parallel.

60

Do these exercises a few times every day before you start skiing, with or without supervision – while you are waiting for the lesson to start for instance, just as a footballer exercises while he's waiting for the game to begin. Stiff muscles are the cause of most early-morning accidents. A few physical exercises loosen you up for action.

After the first two or three lessons are behind you, there are other exercises that will prove useful.

(f) Once you have accomplished simple movements on the slope, run downhill without sticks, hands out at the sides for balance. Keep to a lower part of a slope that ends in a level and uncrowded area.

(g) A popular exercise is running downhill under a series of three or four 'bridges' made of three ski sticks. Squat down to duck under each bridge, stand upright again while approaching the next, duck under it, etc.

(h) Put a descending line of sticks in the snow running downhill at about ten feet intervals. Then weave downhill in and out of the line, making continuous snowplough turns in a simple slalom.

(i) During a traverse, make a small jump with parallel skis to a slightly lower line of traverse, bringing the heels down hard and slowing the forward movement.

During the school skiing trip you may find that instruction is given only during the morning. Informal afternoon skiing can be made great fun and prove useful in building your skill if exercises *(f)*, *(g)* and *(h)* are done by small groups of beginners – but use only the lower few metres of the slope so that emergency stops are easily made.

81. Knees raised jumps on the spot.

82. A real muscle-stretcher. Sit on the heels and stand several times – using no hands or sticks.

64

83, 84. Jumping into the skis-apart or snowplough position and back to the skis-together stance.

85, 86. Rolling round from the waist.

87, 88. Skiing downhill under gates made of ski sticks. Crouch down to get under, then stand up before the next one, before you crouch down again. A good class exercise.

6. Taking a School Party

A Chapter for Teachers/Party leaders

It is perhaps one of the most exciting ventures in school life, not only for the children, for whom a colourful and exotic snow holiday is probably a new experience, but for the teacher who organises and takes the party to the snow. This chapter is primarily directed towards the teacher who may be considering taking a school party to the snow, and who may not have done so previously. The information and suggestions here are by no means comprehensive, but will serve as a pointer to the type of questions that have to be answered, and to the broad lines of pre-trip planning.

The most obvious, though often neglected, maxim is – start planning in time. Start a year ahead. If the course of lessons on the slopes at the resort is to be during the Easter holidays, start your own investigations as early as the previous March or April. Here are a number of suggestions for a teacher's programme during the twelve months up to the school ski course at a resort. More detailed sources of information are listed on page 96. (Further Reading).

MARCH

* Request brochures from tour operators dealing in school party travel to the snow.
* Select region and resort.
* Book provisionally.

Several factors will determine the choice of resort – length of stay coupled with the cost of tour, type of accommodation, type of slopes, numbers in party, age groups, mixed or single sexes, numbers of teachers available etc. Most school-party tour operators know the types of questions that will be asked and their brochures answer the more obviously important ones.

In these days of forced economy the length of the tour will probably be a single week or eight days, which usually allows for just six days – or even six mornings, of tuition. The cost of the tour will depend on which resort and country is chosen. Austria, for instance, used to be the almost automatic choice, now it is amongst the most expensive, while Spain and Italy are usually better value. Bulgaria and Rumania may also be worth investigating as their skiing facilities, though fairly primitive at the moment, are improving. Switzerland is sophisticated but expensive in the known resorts.

The number of initial applications will probably far exceed the final number of the party, and the final figure may be governed by the number of teachers interested in going on the trip. Age groups may be determined by the type of school. Mixed sexes need a male and a female teacher, or a husband-and-wife supervisory team.

Costs for the tour may be a pitfall for the party leaders. We print here a summary of 'What the Price Includes' from a leading schools tour operator as a guide to the cost-inclusions of a reputable company.

What the price includes

Tours begin and end at the airport specified, namely Heathrow, Luton, Gatwick or Manchester. When coach transfers to or from a U.K. airport are ordered, the home terminal may be the School Gate or any other address requested.

Air/Coach tours or All-Coach tours are assumed to originate or to terminate within a radius of 25 miles of central London. Economic add-on fares are offered for these types of tour, to schools located outside this circle.

The following services are included

Travel from and back to the point of origin as defined above, including coach transfers between the foreign airport and the hotel.

In-flight catering as appropriate to the time of travel. A full meal service is provided from the time the journey begins, throughout the tour.

British and foreign airport tax, landing charges and direction control fees.

Government and local tourist taxes, motorway tolls, hotel service charges, etc, including VAT or its equivalent in the country concerned. *It is intended that the party shall be relieved of all kinds of petty payments for the duration of the tour.*

Accommodation with full board for eight days (seven nights).

Hire of good quality skis, sticks and boots for the period of the tour abroad.

Daily ski lessons of two × 2 hours per day. An '8-day' tour with seven nights accommodation will normally have six days' tuition.

The services of representatives at U.K. airports. The services of interpreter-couriers throughout the whole of the stay abroad.

Insurance cover against expense caused through illness, accident or related incidents.

Expenses relating to the provision of a collective passport with visa where necessary.

A detailed itinerary, luggage labels, lapel badges. Collecting cards are available without charge, on request.

Items not included

British coach transfers (to and from U.K. airports). Quotations for this service will be given on request.

Wine and other drinks at the hotel(s) other than at breakfast.

Insurance against loss of ski or other equipment taken on hire when abroad.

British Government Levy of 2%.

Other costs not usually included are third party cover (protecting teacher, school and education authority) cancellation of tour cover, insurance of hired equipment, baggage.

The cost of the party leader or leaders – one to twelve pupils should not be exceeded – is of course affected by the number of free places offered by the tour operator. The normal offer of a free party leader's place is between 1 to 10, and to 15 children.

Additional costs, over the tour operator's quotation, will include transport from local area to tour transport, and cost of dry slope lessons.

MAY

∗   Tour publicity and promotion.
∗   Meeting of interested pupils and parents.
∗   Lecture or film showing region and typical activities.
∗   List of children making up party.

By Spring publicity material, made by interested children themselves perhaps, and displayed boldly on the noticeboard, should be in full swing. A meeting with parents should be set up and leaflets with outline information distributed – dates, total costs, venue, suggested pocket money, necessary clothing and kit, baggage limitations etc., and informing them that skiing is an energetic sport requiring considerable pre-ski training.

Display material will inevitably attract latecomers, and a second parent-child-teacher meeting should be arranged to accommodate them.

JULY

∗ Open a bank account in school name.
∗ Request deposits and consent form.
∗ Check the locality of a ski-clothing hire shop. Inform parents, who should visit it before September and reserve appropriate clothing. If this is delayed it is possible that clothing will be unobtainable at a later date. Shop managers will often be glad to talk to parents at the school.
∗ Organise an evening demonstration of clothing and kit for parents. This will let them know the exact type of clothing necessary and remove several worries.

A deposit-and-consent form from parents will bring the provisional party list into a more concrete form.

Projects such as the history of the region to be visited, its traditions, topography, language (and common phrases) maintain interest during later months.

SEPTEMBER

∗ Commence artificial slope course. (1)

It has been found that a September start at artificial slope lessons has often promoted children to intermediate classes before they ski on snow. When applying for a course remember that the slope will have only a skeleton staff on duty in the summer. Put in a stamped self-addressed envelope. Ask about the price, the duration and the number of pupils to a class (14 should be maximum), and ask to be told the contents of each lesson.

NOVEMBER

  ✳   Collect remainder of money and arrange to handle pocket money.
  ✳   Check or arrange passports.

To speed the passage of groups through passport control, school groups, particularly younger ones, are often included on a collective passport, accepted in most European countries.

JANUARY

  ✳   Commence fitness course and pre-ski exercises.
  ✳   Commence or arrange artificial slope course (2).
  ✳   Check clothes and kit.

Pre-ski exercises have been covered in an earlier chapter, and it is suggested that such a course starts before the artificial slope skiing course. Ideally the fitness course should begin some eight weeks before the party is due to depart, and the artificial ski slope course as close to the date of departure as conveniently possible. However if it can be arranged – and afforded – an earlier artificial slope course of around three lessons, as well as a final one, is strongly recommended.

What to take? Costly clothes are not essential. Although many skiers spend a great deal on their clothes, first-timers who may not take up skiing as a regular sport may wish to hire their kit in U.K. There are a number of reputable companies who hire anoraks, pants, ski-suits – and most of them allow the skier to buy any item for the purchase price less the hiring fee on his return. Tour operators can supply details. So for the skiing part of the trip the essentials are;

Ski pants (not jeans).
Anorak (not motor-cycling jackets, sailing jackets, parkas, as these are not designed for snow).
2 pairs socks.
1 pair gloves (mitts without separate fingers if possible, not knitted gloves).
Goggles or sunglasses.
2 shirts/blouses.
2 sweaters (high-necked if possible).

72

Tights, long underpants or old pyjama trousers (avoid nylon).

Non-skiing gear should be normal for travel that involves visiting a cold climate, and for a holiday which will include some evening social activity.

Select no more than will go into a single case and a small rucksack, apart from the clothes to be worn on the journey.

FEBRUARY

∗   Issue information details and itinerary.
∗   Final meeting before journey.
∗   Medical inspection (2-3 days before leaving).

Detailed information sheets both for children and parents are issued a few weeks before leaving, giving hotel names, location, party leaders' names, telephone numbers at resorts, exact times of departure, and other relevant information.

During a final meeting any late queries can be answered.

A medical inspection that declares children free from communicable disease and fit to travel on the proposed trip is advisable. The doctor's signature on the parental consent form is the usual way of recording the examination.

At the resort

The way in which children behave at a resort reflects upon their school, their town and their country. Fleeting impressions by people of other nationalities on holiday at the resort – however mistaken they may be – are often the only criteria upon which a whole nation or generation is judged. The efficiency of the party leader in handling excited children is obviously of prime importance on such a trip and can determine the success or failure of the ski tour in terms of both educational value and recreation. It should be no surprise (but always is!) to learn that far from being the unruliest of European children, British school parties are considered so well-behaved that in many cases hotel prices are actually reduced for them.

Arrival at the resort signals the end of what has probably been a long and tiring journey, but there is one vital job to be done before settling in. The hotel is likely to be in something of a turmoil, with everybody arriving the same day to start their skiing, and an efficient party leader will find the party's rooms and

73

beds as quickly as possible, jettison everything – and get down to the ski-depot as soon as humanly possible, to be the first to collect skis boots and sticks.

First-day chaos at these places can be imagined, and the earlier groups to be fitted will naturally get the best service.

Party leaders should be active at the shop or depot checking that boots are well fitting and comfortable. Half-a-dozen youngsters whose boots feel as though they have been hired from the Spanish Inquisition can waste a lot of time during the next few days. Bindings will be adjusted at the shop but the leader should, if qualified, re-check releases before anyone puts ski to snow. If the party leader is not familiar with the bindings he should insist that the instructor makes a full check before starting lessons. The length of the ski is of prime importance and should measure at most up to the user's eyebrows. The shorter the ski the easier the beginner will find his turns – and probably the faster he will learn to ski.

89. British school parties arrive at the slopes for the first time, at one of Switzerland's 160 ski schools.

Sticks of the right length are important (they should reach up to the elbow when stuck in the snow) and it's useful to have small self-adhesive labels with the children's names on to attach to the ski sticks. If sticks are mixed up some children may be put at risk, using sticks of the wrong length. All skis are numbered. Children should memorise the last three numbers.

To save possible argument it is advisable to check the type of equipment that will be supplied by the local ski shop well before setting out. However, if the cost of the tour has been shaved for economy reasons, one may find that older equipment is offered. Leather boots are fairly satisfactory, providing they

90. First day. A class learns to snowplough.

don't look like the bottom of a canoe (i.e. they must have a flat sole) but lace-up boots, and cable bindings are not suitable.

That part of the tour which is concerned with skiing itself also needs the close support and co-operation of teachers (in addition to local instructors) although teachers will not of course be asked to display their prowess at the sport or to demonstrate in any way. They may choose to join the class on the slope, or take a watching brief.

In either case it is highly recommended that all party leaders take the *Ski-Parties Organisers Course* offered by the NSFGB and the regional associations in Britain. These are 2-day courses dealing with ski-party organisation and practice, and a growing number of educational authorities are permitting only teachers who hold a certificate to organise and conduct ski-parties. Specific skiing skills are not demanded by the course, but many of the hazards of such a tour may be avoided by attending one.

The need for such courses is becoming increasingly important for these reasons:

1. Up to the present most teachers have become party leaders by assisting senior colleagues. Rapid growth of school ski-parties has created a demand which has exceeded supply through this means.
2. A ski tour is expensive. Qualified leaders are able to ensure their pupils get the full value of the course.
3. The need for higher safety standards in mountainous regions during winter. In the past the conditions of Alpine winters have been under-estimated.

The course includes practical ski instruction, theory relating to bindings, care of skis, clothing, resort selection, fitness, discipline, safety etc.

Advice on courses may be given by the Secretary of the Regional Association (see under artificial slopes page 90) or the P.E. Adviser.

91. Sticks of the right length are important. This young instructor shows the correct height – up to the elbow. Labelling sticks may save accidents with mixed-up lengths.

7. Safe Skiing

Every new skier expects to take a few knocks and tumbles. It is very much part of the fun of learning. But as the number of inexperienced skiers increase year by year a pattern of more serious skiing accidents has emerged. There are two peak periods of danger; when you are first on the slopes in the morning, muscles still stiff and tense; and after a period of intense activity, when muscles have become tired. Ninety per cent of accidents occur during this last period.

So those morning exercises in Chapter 5 are important; they help to limber up muscles which are about to be put to rigorous tests. And it is also important to recognise the point at which muscles have done enough for the day. Give up skiing then, and start walking back.

Many collisions, broken bones or strained muscles could be avoided by following the simple safety rules of skiing.

Getting fit before you go is obviously important. In addition to an artificial slope course and pre-ski exercises, practice the art of climbing stairs – avoid lifts and escalators to strengthen legs that will be taking a lot of punishment later.

Here are some of the simple rules to observe when on the piste

* The slowest skier always has right of way.
* You'll notice that skiers keep clear of your group class. When you are skiing unsupervised avoid groups under instruction, and any skier who looks less accomplished than yourself. It is the responsibility of the better skier to avoid the less proficient.
* If you fall on the piste move rapidly off the run itself so that following

78

skiers, who may be novices, do not have to manoeuvre around you.

* Look around you before you start off again after a halt or a fall, and check constantly that your way ahead is clear.
* Overtake wide, and on the upper side of other skiers; don't cross their possible tracks.
* Never walk on a piste. The holes made by boots can be dangerous to skiers.
* Don't allow your speed to get out of control. Falls at speed can be made by sitting down sideways on your bottom, but it is better not to have to risk injury through sudden stops or windmilling skis.
* Don't ski on slopes marked with a closed sign – *Fermée, Geschlossen, Chiusa* etc.
* Never ski alone away from the main slopes, even when you feel that you are completely proficient. One may need a companion in an emergency.
* If someone is injured do not try to remove clothing or straighten limbs that could be broken. Make the casualty as comfortable as possible and send or go for help, leaving a fit person with the injured skier. Keep him warm.

The rules of the mountain are regarded in most Alpine countries as part of a code, similar to our Highway Code, and must be observed as such.

8. Ski Tests

Most skiers, once they have spent some time on snow, wish to measure their progress against an accepted standard. The British Junior Alpine Ski Tests are now recognised as the standard assessment for skiing proficiency in Great Britain. Devised by the National Ski Federation of Great Britain they may be taken by any skier under the age of 18 on an artificial slope or on snow.

The One Star Test is an elementary test designed to assess proficiency after a short period of training such as a single holiday.

One Star Test

1. Climbing. Side step.
2. Descent. Straight schuss.
3. Snowplough glide descent to a controlled stop.
4. Diagonal traverse to left and right.
5. Four linked consecutive right and left snowplough or basic swing turns.
6. Ski Educational questions (taken from Ski Education leaflet).

Two Star Test

1. Direct controlled side-slip of at least 5 metres in either direction.
2. Diagonal controlled side-slip of at least 5 metres in either direction.
3. 4-6 consecutive basic swing or parallel turns.
4. Non-stop no falls descent through at least 6 open gates.
5. Swing to the slope to a stop from a steep traverse to left and right.
6. Ski Educational questions (taken from Ski Education leaflet).

Three Star Test – advanced skiing test

Note: The candidate must show throughout this test that he/she can ski to a good parallel standard. The turns must be smooth with no sign of stemming whatsoever. So long as the skis remain parallel throughout all the turns they may be held in slight open stance (the parallel turns may be done with or without a small hop).

1. 4 long continuous parallel turns with stick (this means that the candidate should make full use of the width and length of the slope).
2. 4 long continuous turns without sticks.
3. 8-12 linked continuous short parallel turns (these may be done in short swing or in wedeln style).
4. 8-12 single gate slalom run down slope.
   No fall descent through the gates.
   (The person organising the test can judge the slalom run against time if he so wishes).
5. Ski Educational questions (taken from Ski Education leaflet).

Three Star Test on snow slopes only.

9. Ski-words

Abonnement	A season ticket for lifts or lessons.
Artificial slope	Nylon or other plastic surface laid on sloping ground and used for teaching and practice.
Bindings	Metal or plastic systems that secure the boot to the ski. They consist of a toe and a heel binding. Both have a safety release system which should be carefully tested before use.
Cable car	German, *drahtseilbahn;* French *téléferique;* Italian *teleferica.* A large closed 'car' suspended from an endless motorised cable used to convey up to 100 people from one mountain station to another.
Chair lift	German *sessellift;* French *télé-siege;* Italian *seggiovia.* A suspended 'garden-seat' for one or two passengers attached to an endless motorised cable. Often used for conveying skiers in winter and tourists in summer, they usually afford a good view of the countryside.
Drag lift	German *skilift;* French *télé-ski;* Italian *sciovia.* And endless cable from which run sprung cables at intervals, down to ground level, and ending in a bar shaped like a T or disc which skiers hold and are towed uphill on their skis. Using a drag lift needs a little instruction; the T-bar takes two at a time. It is safer for beginners if they are about the same size and weight.

92. A swiss cable car over the high slopes.

93. An opportunity for these chair lift passengers to enjoy fine scenery in the Swiss mountains.

94. Drag lift with T-bar, familiarly known as a meat-hook.

Edges, edging:	Metal edges run along each side of a ski; they are L-shaped in section to give a 'cutting edge' to the ski. The skier 'bites' the edges into a slope during a traverse to prevent them slipping sideways downhill, and during a stem to apply a braking effect.
Fall Line	An imaginary line running downhill the steepest way from any given point.
Gondola telecabin	German *gondelbahn*; French *telecabine*; Italian *telecabine*. A small cable car for two or four passengers, often in the shape of a closed carriage.

95. A gondola or telecabine traverses the dizzy heights of the Alps.

Graduated Length Method	A system of teaching skiing by using ultra-short skis 1 metre long, graduating to 135 cm and then to 160 cm skis. Parallel skiing is taught from the start and this method is a rapid way of learning, mainly as short skis do not encourage a beginner to go too quickly, and turning is much easier than on a long ski. Called GLM in the in the United States, Ski Evolutif in France.
Mogul	Small hillocks or bumps that are created in the ski fields by skiers constantly taking the same line in turning through a slope.
Nordic Skiing	German *langlauf;* French *ski de fond.* The original type of skiing, used for getting from one place cross-country to

96. Ski touring, trail-skiing, langlauf, ski de fond, Nordic skiing call it what you like, it is rapidly becoming a popular family sport.

another by walking on skis. In the Alps skiiers travel along marked trails, mainly over flat or undulating country. Skis are narrower than those used in downhill skiing, and boots are not as heavy or rigid. This type of skiing is rapidly becoming very popular amongst holidaymakers in the Alpa.

Parablacks	Shaped plastic 'boxes' fitted to the top of each ski about a foot from the tip to prevent skis crossing, particularly in deep snow.
Piste	Marked runs used by most skiers. The beginners piste or nursery slope is usually wide, always gentle, and has a roomy flat area at its base.
Running surface	That part of the ski in contact with the snow. It has a central groove running along the entire length, helping directional stability.
Schuss	Skiing straight down the hill, or fall line, with skis parallel.
Slalom	A downhill race weaving through a line of sticks or a series of open 'gates'.
Stem	A skiing movement in which the skier travels downhill with skis spread in a V formation, tips close and heels wide. The first slowing-down or stopping method taught to a beginner.
Sticks, poles	Light, strong metal sticks (sometimes wooden sticks are issued on the artificial slope) used to facilitate turning and walking on skis. Baskets are fitted a few inches above the lower pointed ends to prevent them sinking too deeply into the snow.
Wedel, wedeln	Short, fast consecutive parallel turns made by an advanced downhill skier.

Appendix.
Organisations and Addresses

The National Ski Federation of Great Britain
118 Eaton Square, London SW1W 9AF

This is the governing body of skiing in U.K. and comprises member clubs, individual life members and affiliated members. The NSFGB is responsible for all skiing activities in U.K., for the promotion of British skiing as a sport and the selection and training of teams for major world contests.

The Ski Club of Great Britain, 118 Eaton Square, London SW1W 9AF

The national club for skiers. For three quarters of a century it has promoted skiing in all its forms and it provides unique advantages to its 23,000 Members and 120 affiliated clubs and schools.

Such unbiased and informative advice on resorts and equipment can be found nowhere else; special holiday and travel schemes are great money-savers; skiing parties with a purpose take all ages and standards – children, beginners, experts – everyone can have a really good holiday while improving their skiing; SCGB Reps in major alpine resorts take members skiing – different standards each day – run tests and competitions – hold parties. Back in Britain 45 local reps hold filmshows, artificial slope courses, parties – all round the country.

There is Grass skiing at a dozen hillsides round Britain every summer weekend with racing and competitions at all levels, and the magazine *Ski Survey*, free to Members three times a year has all the latest on every aspect of skiing. Borrow Ski-Talk, a ten-minute film all about the Club.

ARTIFICIAL SKI SLOPES IN U.K.

(with catchment area and regional ski association secretary)

London and South East Region Ski Association
(covers London, Surrey, Sussex, Kent)

Hon. (Act.) Secretary – Miss Veronica Barnes, c/o S.C.G.B.

Alexandra Palace Ski Centre, Alexandra Park, London N22 4AY.
   Tel. (01) 888 2284/5.

Watford Ski School, Woodside Playing fields, Horseshoe Lane, Garston, Watford, Herts. WD2 7HH.
   Tel. Garston (Herts.) 76559 (24 hrs.), 76550.

Sandown Ski Schools Limited, Sandown Park, More Lane, Esher, Surrey.
   Tel. Esher 65588/67132.

Crystal Palace National Sports Centre, Norwood, London SE19.
   Tel. (01) 778 0131.

Lords Ski School Limited, Lords Ground, St. John's Wood, London NW8 8QN.
   Tel. (01) 286 4535.

Bowles Outdoor Pursuits Centre, Eridge, Nr. Tunbridge Wells, Kent, TN3 9LW.
   Tel. Crowborough 4127.

Sports & Leisure Ski School, Sussex.

Folkestone Sports Centre, Radnor Park Avenue, Folkestone, Kent.
   Tel. Folkestone 58222/3.

Woolwich Garrison, Greenhill Terrace, London, SE18.

Guildford Church of England Secondary School, Surrey.

Warley Ski School, Warley Sports Centre, Holdens Wood, Warley Gap, Brentwood, Essex.
   Tel. Brentwood 211994.

90

Southern Region Ski Association (For: Berks., Bucks., Hants., Oxfordshire)

Hon. Secretary   Mr Derek Abbott, TAAB Laboratories, 52 Kidmore End Road, Emmer Green, Reading, Berks.
   Tel. Reading 475388.

Stainforth Ski School, Hurst Road, Aldershot, Hants.
   Tel. Aldershot 24431 Ext. 2299.

Southampton Ski Slope, The Sports Centre, Bassett, Southampton, Hants.
   Tel. Southampton 68598.

Brize Norton Ski Centre, Oxon.

Calshot Activities Centre, Calshot Spit, Southampton, Hants.
   Tel. Fawley 892077.

Bulmershe Ski Slope, Berks.

Carter & Sons Limited, Berkshire.

Eastleigh Sports Centre, Hants.

South West Ski Association (for Wiltshire, Gloucestershire, Dorset, Somerset, Devon, Cornwall)

Hon. Secretary   Mr John Hodge, The Sports Council, 17 The Square, Crewkerne, Somerset.
   Tel. Crewkerne 3491.

Exeter & District Ski Club, Clifton Hill Sports Centre, Exeter, Devon.
   Tel. Axminster 33377.

Wellington Sports Centre, Somerset.

Wessex Ski Association, Devon.

Bryant Outdoor Centre, Colston Street, Bristol, BS1 5BY.
   Tel. Bristol 23166.

Eastern Region (for Beds., Hunts., Suffolk, Norfolk, Essex, Cambs., Herts.)

NSFGB Representative   Mr I. Palfrey, Solar Via, Happisburgh, Norwich, Norfolk.

Welwyn Garden City Ski Centre, Gosling Stadium, Stanborough Road, Welwyn Garden City, Herts.
Tel. Welwyn Garden City 29025.

Basildon Ski Centre, Basildon.

Wensum Lodge Ski Slope, Lower King Street, Norwich, Norfolk.
Tel. Walcott 442.

The Ski Centre, Harlow Sports Centre, Hammarskjold Road, Harlow, Essex.
Tel. Harlow 21792.

West Midlands Ski Association (for Shropshire, Stafford, Hereford, Worcester, Warwick)

Hon. Secretary   Mr David Francis, The Sports Council, Crest House, 7 Highfield Road, Edgbaston, Birmingham, B15 3EG.

Kidsgrove Ski Centre, Stoke on Trent.

Hard's Birmingham Ski School, Birmingham.

Birmingham Ski School, The Mountain Shop, 18-19, Snow Hill, Queensway, Birmingham, B46 ER.
Tel. (021) 236 6816.

Court Centre, Madeley, Telford, Shropshire.
Tel. Telford 585823.

Dudley Ski Centre, Worcs.

Tebbutt's Ski School, 42 High Bullen, Wednesbury, S. Staffs.
Tel. (Ski shop hours) (021) 556 0802.

East Midlands Ski Association (for Derby [less Peak District], Nottingham [less Lindsey], Leicester, Rutland, Northampton)

Hon. Secretary   Dr J. G. Elder Smith, Tristans, Grandfield Crescent, Radcliffe-on-Trent, Nottingham.

Carlton Forum Ski Slope, Coningswath Road, Carlton, Nottingham, NG4 3SH. Tel. Nottingham 872333.

Skew Bridge Ski Club, Northants.

Yorkshire and Humberside Ski Federation (for East & West Yorkshire, and Lindsey, Lincs.)

Hon. Secretary   Mr Ivor Davies, 50 Turnsteads Avenue, Cleckheaton, Yorkshire.

Catterick Ski Slope, Loos Road, Catterick Garrison, Yorkshire. Tel. Catterick Camp 2521, Slope Ext. 282 Bookings Ext. 7022.

Centresport Ski School, Centresport (Leeds Ltd) 40 Woodhouse Lane, Leeds. Tel. Leeds 42079.

North East Ski Association (for Northumberland, Durham, North Yorkshire)

Hon. Secretary   Mr W. Hall, 3 Valley Close, Tow Law, Co. Durham. Tel. (038) 885 248.

Northumberland Ski Slope, Cottingwood Lane, Morpeth, Northumberland. Enquiries to Education Dept., Eldon House, Regents Centre, Gosforth, Newcastle.   Tel. Gosforth 850181.

Seaburn Ocean Park Ski Slope, Co. Durham.

North West Ski Federation (for Lancashire, Cheshire, Derby [Peak District])

Hon. Secretary   Mr Derek Lunt, 20 Aldwych Road, Liverpool 12. Tel. (051) 228 7622.

Ski Rossendale, Oakenhead Wood, Haslingden Old Road, Rawtenstall, Rosendale.   Tel. Rossendale 28844.

Squash Ski Runcorn, Palace Fields, Runcorn, Cheshire, WA7 2PT.
   Tel. Runcorn 64104.

Counthill School Slope, c/o Amenities & Recreation Dept., Alexandra Park,
   Oldham, Lancs.
   Tel. (061) 624 9993.

Pendle Ski Club, Lancs.

Physical Education Department, Lancaster.

Manchester Ski School, Ellis Brigham, 6-14 Cathedral Street, Manchester.
   Tel. (061) 834 0161.

Kirkby Ski Slope, Kirkby.

Indoor Sports, Cheshire.

Oval Sports Centre, Cheshire.

Northern Ski Federation (for Cumbria)

Hon. Secretary   Miss N. E. E. Smith, 3 The Hawthorns, Keswick,
   Cumberland.
   Tel. Keswick 72799.

Carlisle & District Ski Club, Edenside, Carlisle, Cumbria.
   Tel. Bookings to Weheral 60244.

West Cumberland Ski Club, Cumberland.

Ski Council of Wales

Hon. Secretary   Mr Fairfax Luxmoore, Castell Howard, Llandysul, Dyfed,
   Wales.
   Tel. Pontshaen 209.

Plas-y-Brenin National Mountaineering Centre, Capel Curig, Betwys-Y-Coed,
   Caerns.
   Tel. Capel Curig 214.

Cardiff Ski Centre, Cardiff.

Black Mountain Ski Slope, Powys.

94

The Sports Centre, Pontypool, Monmouthshire.
 Tel. Pontypool 56955.

Kelsterton College, Flints.

The Ski Slope, Brecon.

The Scottish National Ski Council

Secretary & Treasurer   Guy Chilver-Stainer, The Barn, Balmore-by-Torrance,
 Glasgow, Scotland.
 Tel. Balmore 496.

Hillend Ski Centre, Biggar Road, Edinburgh, EH10 7DU.
 Tel. (031) 445 4433.

Kaimhill Ski Slope, Aberdeen.

Polmonthill Ski Centre, Polmont Farm, Polmont, Stirlingshire.
 Tel. Polmont 3660.

Bearsden Ski Club, The Mound, Stockiemuir Road, Courthill, Bearsden,
 Glasgow.
 Tel. (041) 942 2933.

Ancrum Activities Centre, Dundee.

Newmilns Ski Slope, Ayrshire.

Fife Institute of Physical & Recreational Education, Fife.

Ulster Ski Federation

Hon. Secretary   c/o Ian McIntyre, Plycol – Montgomerie (N.I.) Ltd, Falcon
 Road, Belfast B212 6RB.

Castle Robin Ski Slope, Co. Antrim.

Ski and Golf Centre, Co. Armagh.

Physical Education Centre, Belfast.

Craigavon Golf and Ski Centre, Silverwood, Lurgan, Craigavon, Co. Armagh.
 Tel. Lurgan 6606.

Further Reading

For school children or party leaders

Books
Going Ski-ing by Alan Gibbon.
We Learned to Ski (Sunday Times)
Pre-Ski Exercises Published by the Ski Club of Great Britain
Getting in Shape to Ski by Tage Pederson
Ski Teaching by John Shedden
Know the Game Skiing Published by EP Publishing Ltd

Magazines

Ski Magazine (Monthly September-February – available at bookstalls)
Ski Survey (Ski Club members free. Also available at bookstalls)